AF682387

Hansel and Gretel in the Deep Online Forest

A Coloring Cyber Literacy Story

Sandra Estok

Copyright © 2020 by Sandra Estok, MBA, GIAC-GSLC, CIPM – Founder of Way2Protect

Story Adaptation by Elisha Fernández and Sandra Estok

Developmental Editing and Story Strategy by Elayna Fernández

Illustrations by Elisha Fernández

Cover design by SocialClose Media Agency with Illustration by Elisha Fernández

Published by thePositiveMOM.com

All rights reserved

To my brothers Edward and Camilo.
I love you!

Once upon a time, there was a family that consisted of a mom, a dad, and their two twin children, Hansel and Gretel.

The parents were extremely busy, both working full time jobs and spending time at the office after business hours regularly.

They were not able to spend as much time with their children as they would have liked. They left in the morning before Hansel and Gretel woke up, and came home late at night.

Hansel and Gretel were as close as a 13-year-old brother and sister could be. They relied on each other, especially since their parents were not home most of the time.

They woke up on their own, Hansel would prepare lunch for the both of them, and after getting ready and eating breakfast, they would walk to the bus stop together and go to school. Once they got home, Hansel and Gretel would do homework, chores, and play with toys and in the online forest before going to bed.

Hansel and Gretel's parents had taught them to be cyber savvy, and they were naturals at using their computers and phones.

However, even though Hansel and Gretel were smart children, the parents worried about the children being alone all day, especially since they had heard rumors about kids getting lost in the dangerous, deep online forest.

"We have to work to make our home payment, pay the utilities, buy groceries, and make sure our kids have a good education. How could we know if our kids are spending their time in the deep online forest? How can we keep them safe even if we're not home?" said the mother to the father.

The father had heard of parenting tools they could install for their home network. That way, they could limit where Hansel and Gretel would play and how long and, hopefully, reduce any risks of potential danger. They decided to investigate together.

One Sunday afternoon, the only day Hansel and Gretel's parents had a short break from work, they started researching online parental tools. They found a handful that sounded helpful and were reading different benefits and features out loud.

Hansel overheard their parents talking about the parenting "control" tools, and, alarmed, he immediately told Gretel.

Hansel and Gretel were already very computer savvy! They navigated the online forest frequently, and although they had never been in the deepest part of the forest, they had heard horrible stories: kids getting lost, families losing their house, their money being stolen, and even their own names!

These stories frightened Hansel and Gretel - like their mom and dad, they wanted their family to always be safe and united.

However, the kids didn't want to stop going to the online forest. It was just so big and beautiful! Some of the areas were surrounded by flowers and pretty trees, and when you search for something you want or need, you can almost always easily find it.

Hansel and Gretel didn't like the idea of these controlling tools, so on Monday, they decided to enter the deep online forest once again to play games and browse.

They logged onto the computer together and entered one of their favorite chatrooms. No sooner than they had logged in, did they receive a message from someone they didn't know.

"Click on this link now!" the mystery sender insisted.

Then Hansel and Gretel started receiving emails, text messages and multiple invites on their Fairybook (a popular social media site), about a MAGICAL game in the deep online forest.

All they had to do was click on the link to be instantly transported to a sweet area, full of colors, fun games, and cool prizes.

fairybook
You have seven
new invitations!
7

It was said to be a place where kids could play and do anything they wanted, and in this amazing place "all their wishes would come true!"

Up until now Hansel and Gretel had hesitated because their parents told them to be cautious when something appeared to be too good to be true.

However, the latest message clearly said that this would be their LAST chance to get to this wonderful location in the deep online forest! It was hard to resist!

Little did Hansel and Gretel know that behind that link to access the magical game lived the wicked Cybermonsters.

fairybook messaging
This is your LAST CHANCE to visit the magical online forest. All your wishes will come true!
Click the link *here* NOW for fun games, cool prizes, and more!

Once kids enter Cybermonster territory by clicking the link, all their information, pictures, friend contacts and anything else they have in their device becomes haunted and their technology can no longer be used, and they can't break the spell unless their family pays a very high price.

Right before Hansel and Gretel decided to click on the link, something amazing happened. Both of their parents called them from work to check in on them!

Hansel and Gretel decided to tell their parents about how they were about to click the link to get access to the online deep forest.

They confessed that even though they were hesitant before,the thought of having parental controls made them feel like they could no longer have fun in the online forest and they had FOMO (Fear of Missing Out).

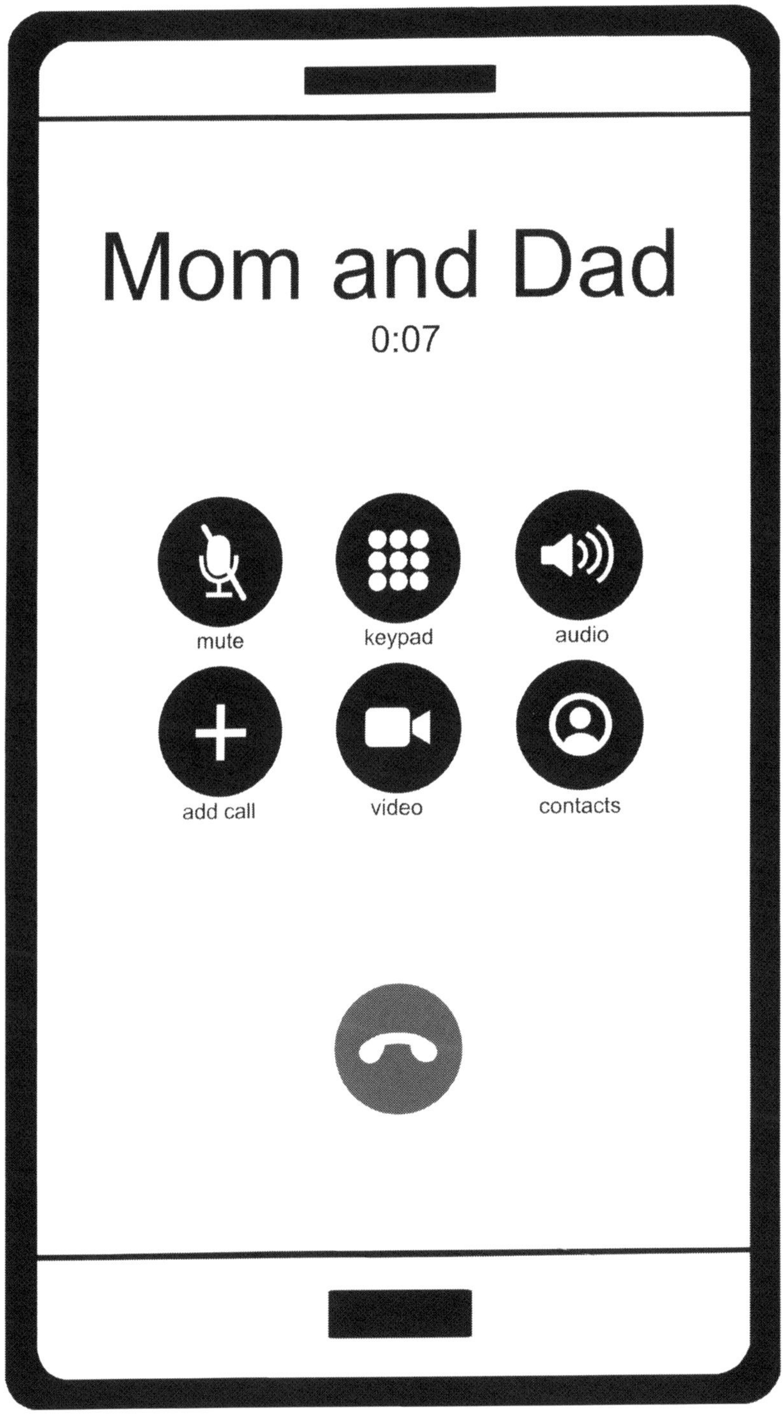
Mom and Dad
0:07
mute
keypad
audio
add call
video
contacts

When the parents got home, they decided to enjoy a special night, talking about cyber safety. The parents hugged Hansel and Gretel and thanked them for their honesty and for not clicking the link.

Their mom said:

"I assure you that your dad and I have done a lot of research on parental tools."

"Yes and while these tools keep bad and dangerous places away, all the other fun activities you enjoy in the online forest can still be accessed," explained their dad.

Hansel and Gretel understood that the tools would protect them, and that they still had the responsibility to remain vigilant because clicking on any Cybermonster's link could be devastating to their family's safety.

Their parents could do their best to protect Hansel and Gretel, but they wouldn't be stepping in and making all their cyber decisions for them. They told the kids how much they trusted them to make cyber savvy decisions in the online forest.

Hansel and Gretel jumped up and down, full of joy that they could still enjoy what they loved about the online forest.

Happily EVER CYBER

They promised to never click on a link full of promises, open file attachments or accept friend requests especially if they come from a stranger and they promised to share their cyber experiences and questions during their fun family time.

And they all lived Happily Ever Cyber!

Made in United States
Orlando, FL
30 September 2023

37432771R00017